"One Country! One Constitution! One Destiny!"

SPEECHES

OF

WILLIAM CURTIS NOYES, DANIEL S. DICKINSON, AND LYMAN TREMAIN,

AT THE

GREAT UNION WAR RATIFICATION MEETING,

HELD AT THE

COOPER INSTITUTE, IN THE CITY OF NEW YORK

OCTOBER 8th, 1862.

ALSO, THE

SPEECH AND LETTER OF ACCEPTANCE

OF

GEN. JAMES S. WADSWORTH.

ELECTORS OF NEW YORK,

Read, and determine who you will support at the coming Election!

UNION WAR RATIFICATION MEETING.

At 7½ o'clock, the Great Hall of the Institute being then densely packed, Hon. JAMES A. BRIGGS called the meeting to order, and nominated, as PRESIDENT of the meeting, WM. CURTIS NOYES, of whom he spoke as a descendant of a soldier of the Revolution. When the applause which greeted this announcement had subsided, Mr. Noyes, coming forward, spoke as follows:

FELLOW-CITIZENS—I do not feel myself worthy of the approbation with which you have hailed my name; but if I have any claim to your consideration, it is that the person from whom I am descended, and to whom allusion has been made, spilled his blood in the cause of freedom at the battle of Brandywine. (Cheers.) It has not been in my power to make such a sacrifice; but such sacrifices are made all over this country now, and this meeting is for the purpose of stimulating others to make sacrifices in the cause of liberty, and to strengthen the hands of the President of the United States (applause), patriotic and noble as he is in all the measures that characterize his wise administration. (Loud cheers.) I thank you most sincerely for selecting me to preside over this assembly; but it is not my purpose, nor would it be quite proper, to anticipate the graver and wiser discussions which will be had before you. At the same time, you will pardon me for saying that this is not a political meeting, in the ordinary paltry party sense. (Applause.) It is, indeed, political in its aims and aspirations; because it relates to good government, to the preservation of the Constitution, to the sacredness of the Union, and to the preservation of the lives and the property of all Union-loving men. In that sense it is the highest political wisdom which has brought this meeting together, and which in every heart here beats with patriotic impulses in behalf of the country, in behalf of its integrity, in behalf of union for every inch of its soil. (Loud applause.) You are not met merely for the purpose of selecting men, or approving the selection of men that has been already made, for the purpose of aiding the general Government in carrying on this war; but you are met for the purpose of stimulating yourselves and stimulating others who shall hear of the proceedings of this meeting, with new loyalty, with renewed earnestness, and with a devotion to the country which will find no satisfaction unless it be in the removal of every traitor and every rebel from the land. (Enthusiastic cheering.) We are met to tell those who are entrusted with the conduct of public affairs at Washington that they are sustained by a grateful and loyal and self-sacrificing people—(cheeers)—and that any measures which they have inaugurated, or which they may introduce for the purpose of putting down this rebellion, will receive our earnest and continued approbation. (Loud cheers.) You are met to say to the President, and to the army which he commands, that they must go forward, and that millions and millions of hearts all over the country beat in unison with them in support of the great principle of the Declaration of Independence, that heaven-declared doctrine that "all men are created equal." (Rapturous applause. Cries of "That's the talk." Hurra, hurra, hurra.) You are met to support the recent proclamation of the President of the United States—(Renewed and long-continued cheers, most of the audience standing up and giving vent to vociferous demonstrations)—that greatest boon next to the Bible and the Declaration of Independence that was ever given to man (cheers)—a proclamation that will write his name high in the annals of fame throughout all ages. ("Good.") And you are met, too, to endorse that beautiful proclamation of the young general who commands our armies, approving that declaration—(This stirred up the audience again, and brought most of them to their feet, cheering heartily)—a general who, recently, at least, seems to combine the energy, and skill, and courage of youth, with the prudence and discretion of age, and who is to lead our armies, if sustained by the people, as he will be, to victory, conclusive and final. ("Good.") Some of us may have hoped that he had been more active; but, perhaps, the good results which have been achieved, under Providence, could not have been obtained except by the delay which has occurred. And now we shall march on under the proclamation and under his guidance, to victory final and complete, over every rebel in the land. (Cheers. A voice—"Hurra for Fremont." Hisses.) I wish you to recollect also that it is not a party meeting in the sense of its being a meeting of the democratic party, or of the Union party, or of the republican party. It is a meeting of genuine, earnest, positive friends of the country—(cheering)—men earnest and honestly loyal—(good)—men who know no hypocrisy in the expression of their loyalty to their country, who do not say one thing and mean another thing, and who will not be—as a distinguished man said to me to-day—honest before the election, but traitors afterwards. When the democratic party was broken into fragments at Charleston by a band of traitors and conspirators, it crystalized into three classes. I would compare them as good, worse, worst—(laughter)—and in considering them shall reverse the order of the comparison. The worst are the traitors, the conspirators, composing the entire democratic party of the South, now as a general thing, in arms against the country, and headed by their candidate for President, who is engaged in slaughtering some of the men who voted for him, and in denouncing many and many thousands who voted for him. That is the first class—the worst. The next class are those who are worse. They are those who, when Fort Sumter was assailed, and its beleaguered garrison were attempted to be murdered, were cold, indifferent, doubting of success; taking no share in the patriotic excitement which prevailed a year ago last April—taking no pains to stimulate the energies of the country to great activity in the struggle which was upon us, and recently crystalizing into a party opposed to the administration—opposed to the war into which madness and treason have plunged us, and ready to submit to, or to do any thing to gain favor with the rebels, with whom they are affiliated. (Applause.) Not, indeed, that they are all traitors. I do not charge any such thing as that. But I say they are in sympathy with them, that they are willing to submit to their demands, and that some of them—the leaders—would give the rebels a blank sheet of paper on which to write such terms as they might see fit to prescribe. I furnish you a single instance of it. The leader of that party in the city of New York is he who, in the winter of 1861, desired to send arms to the South with which the rebels could fight their Northern neighbors. Many of those who affiliate with the class of which I have spoken, do so in the integrity of their hearts, no doubt, but they are mistaken and deceived. The designs of the leaders are base, disloyal, and they mean nothing less than the prostration of the North and the triumph of the South. And now I come, with great pleasure, to the good class. ("Bravo.") Their representatives are here. Their representatives are all over the country, in those good and loyal democrats, who, as early as the 24th of April, allied themselves with the Union men North, and they have known no faltering from that day to this. (Cheers.) My word for it, they will never falter. ("No, never.") Let me review, for a moment, the antecedents of some of them, for the purpose of showing not only that they are the true representatives of the democracy—that party which was always the party of progress and freedom—but that they are the type of the whole class represented in the great Union party, which is for saving this country and its constitution, in all its benignant integrity. One of them, sitting on my right, was first known to me as a respected State Senator, elected by the democratic party. He was afterwards Lieutenant Governor, then United States Senator, then—by the votes of the Union party last year, to which he readily joined himself—elected to the office he now holds. I allude to Daniel S. Dickinson—(cheers)—able, eloquent, making every sacrifice that could be made to promote the success of the country and urge on the war. You will hear his eloquent voice in support of the great principles for which we are contending. The other; young indeed, but as good a soldier. He represented his party in the councils of the State a few years ago as Attorney-General, and always held a high, commanding and influential position in that party. They sought to bribe him last year by nominating him to the office held by my distinguished friend on my right; but he was insensible to the blandishments of office, and knew his country, only his country—(cheers)—and he declined promptly. He is now here, having lifted his voice, and being again ready to lift his voice, in favor of the country, irrespective of party—irrespective of every party but the party of the Union. I commend the eloquent utterances of these gentlemen to you, to prove not only that the democracy of the country—the loyal democracy—is right, but that with energy in the holiest of causes, success with proper efforts must attend every thing which we do in behalf of the country, now distressed and bleeding from the effects of the rebellion. (Cheers.)

A list of VICE-PRESIDENTS and SECRETARIES was then put in nomination by CHAS. S. SPENCER, Esq., containing the names of many of the most eminent and patriotic citizens of New York, including a large number of War Democrats. After which, JOHN H. WHITE, Esq., presented a series of resolutions, which were adopted with immense applause. Two of them were received by the audience with such marked significance and wild enthusiasm, they are given entire:

Resolved, That, in the emphatic language of ANDREW JOHNSON, "Rebels in arms against the Government have no right to any property." We hold that they cannot invoke the protection of a Constitution which they spurn and repudiate; and we therefore assert that it is the duty of the Government to use all and every appliance in its power to cripple and crush out this mad and unnatural revolt; and in that view we hail with the liveliest satisfaction the recent war proclamation of the President, declaring his intention to emancipate the slaves of all rebels who do not return to their allegiance by the 1st of January, 1863. It cannot hurt loyal citizens; and, judging from the wail that comes from Richmond, it is likely to strike with fatal effect the fountain-head of this rebellion.

Resolved, That it is with mingled feelings of pity and contempt we look upon that uneasy, uncomfortable, and dissatisfied portion of our so-called "fellow-citizens" who spend their time in whining about the right of free speech, and vainly imagine that by THEIR much speaking they may become worthy candidates for Fort Lafayette; the MARK MEDDLES of the community, aching to be kicked into martyrs; full of sound and fury about the rights of the South, but having no word of rebuke for traitors, no denunciation for the brutal and fiendish atrocities perpetrated upon the men and women of the South for having dared to stand by the Union; no sympathy for our noble soldiers now in the field; and no respect for the memory of those brave men who have fallen in defending our time-honored and glorious flag. "*They are joined to their idols; let them alone.*"

The President then introduced DANIEL S. DICKINSON, who, after the cheering had subsided, spoke as follows:

We have been called together, my friends, to ratify or disaffirm the nominations made by the recent Union Convention at Syracuse, and to discuss the claims of the candidates for the stations for which they have been proposed, and the principles upon which they stand before the people, positively, and in contrast with the opposing forces. It is no time for circumlocution, and the more directly the subject is approached the better the issues will be understood.

When the most atrocious conspiracy which ever desecrated earth found development in an assault upon our National flag at Sumter, and in efforts to massacre a half-starved garrison, placed there in a time of profound peace, according to uniform usage, for no other offence than asserting the supremacy of their country's Constitution, and giving to the breeze, as emblematical thereof, the glorious Stars and Stripes of their fathers—when the brave volunteers who were hurrying to the defence of our nation's capital, to save it from mob rule and rebellion and conflagration, were bleeding by traitorous hands—when strong men trembled, when women wept, and children instinctively clung closer to the maternal bosom—when all communication between the loyal States and the capital was cut off by rebellious forces—when the President elect of the United States had then recently reached the seat of Government, where duty called him, by a circuitous and an unusual route, and in disguise, to escape the dagger of the assassin, and when our land was filled with excitement and consternation and alarm—when "shrieked the timid and stood still the brave," and the confiding masses looked about to see who were the men for the crisis, among the citizens of the Empire State, who had borne a part in public affairs and were naturally looked up to as exemplars in such a crisis, there were two whom subsequent events have made conspicuous in domestic history. They did not, like the two characterized by the prophet Nathan, live in one city (laughter); nor was the one rich and the other poor; but neither was far from the central regions of this great State. Both were in the full maturity of natural life; both had been honored by marks of popular confidence; both had been educated by that care known only to a father's solicitude and a father's hope; both were blessed with ample wealth—the fruits of industrious and enterprising progenitors—and both were qualified by circumstances and fortune to exercise an important influence upon public affairs in moments of peril. In this, their country's evil day, both left the State of their birth and residence, and their homes of comfort and plenty, about the same time, and went abroad. One bid adieu to his wife and children, turned his back upon his broad and fertile acres, and his extensive business pursuits, and, with his sons and assistants, repaired to the theater of strife and danger (cheers) while yet the arm of Government was paralyzed by treachery, and destitution reigned in the camp, and ordered forward cargoes of subsistence for famishing soldiers, and with his own hands, and by the aid of his sons, apportioned them among the needy upon the rebellious border. He gave, too, three sons to the cause of the Constitution; he volunteered his own services to the Government for the field, in any capacity where he could be most serviceable in crushing the rebellion (applause); was (entirely unsolicited by him) appointed a Brigadier-General of Volunteers, accepted a commission, and has since devoted his time and energies and ample means to his country's cause, and is at this hour doing service. This man's name is JAMES S. WADSWORTH. [Tremendous applause.]

About the same time the other individual designated left his family and residence of repose, but not for the seat of war. [Laughter.] He hied himself away upon the double-quick in the opposite direction [laughter], and for nearly half a year hid himself among the lakes and rivers and romantic woodlands and inland towns of Wisconsin; and his tongue was as silent on the subject of denouncing the rebellion as those of the murdered volunteers, whose "ghosts walked unrevenged amongst us." [Sensation.] There we may suppose he basked and balanced, and watched and waited, and turned and twisted [laughter], until autumn, when a small knot of defunct, defeated, desperate, and despicable politicians, who had for years hung upon the subsistence department of the Democratic party in this State, came to his relief, by entering the field. [Laughter.] They borrowed without leave the honored name of Democracy, under which to perpetrate their covert treason, as the hypocrite

> "Stole the livery of the court of heaven
> To serve the devil in."

Their disgraceful and disloyal record stands out as the doings of men too stolid in political depravity to be gifted with ordinary instincts, and too regardless of the popular will to be mindful of shame; and the defeat they experienced at the hands of the people, should serve as a warning to trimmers and traitors and parricides and ingrates, through all future time.

This movement drew the secluded one from his hiding place, and he came forth, with all the courage of him who, in a conflict with his wife, being driven under the bed, while remaining thus ensconced, declared, that whether she consented or not, he would look out through a knot-hole in the clapboards, *so long as he had the spirit of a man!* [Great and repeated laughter and applause.] He entered the political canvass, and on the 28th October, 1861, a few days before the election, made a speech, the burden of which was an apology for the rebellion, and a condemnation of the Administration for having meted out the rigor of martial law to those in arms against the Government. Though abounding with flimsy disguises and sophistical generalities, it contained one point worthy of not only notice, but of the severest reprehension, and here it is:

"If it is true that slavery must be abolished to save this Union, THEN THE PEOPLE OF THE SOUTH SHOULD BE ALLOWED TO WITHDRAW THEMSELVES FROM THAT GOVERNMENT which cannot give them the protection guaranteed by its terms."

What! Place this glorious Union—this heritage of human hope—this asylum for the world's weary pilgrim—this refuge for the oppressed of earth, in the scale of being beneath the black and bloated and bloody—the corrupt and corrupting—the stultified and stultifying institution of slavery! No! Sooner than see this Union severed, let not only the institution perish whenever and wherever it can be found, but let the habitations that have known it perish with it, and be known no more forever. [Tremendous and long-continued applause. "That's so." "That's the talk." Three cheers.] And yet this returning fugitive from patriotism proclaims as his creed, in effect if not in terms, that if either slavery or the Union must be destroyed, it should be the Union! And the name of this man is HORATIO SEYMOUR. [Sensation.]

These two men have been placed in nomination by opposing organizations for the office of Governor of this State—the one by the loyal masses, acting as a Union organization, regardless and independent of former political opinion—pledged to the support of the Administration in all just efforts to restore law and order—pledged to every purpose looking to the sure, speedy, unconditional reduction of the Rebellion, and to any and every measure calculated to secure that result at the earliest moment—the destruction of slavery, if necessary, included; the other brought forward by political guerillas, who have crawled from beneath the popular avalanche of last year, to repeat their efforts at imposition, under new and improved disguises—the Peace-party patriots, the ninth-resolution mongers of 1861, the apologists of rebellion, and the villifiers of the Administration, because it had met treason with its half million of armed men in the revolting States, and its spies and pimps, and creeping miscreants in the loyal States (who deserved the jail and the gibbet), with the plenary power of martial law, instead of propositions of peace! On the occasion of his recent nomination by the Albany Convention, of which he was a member, he was most cruelly taken by surprise; he did not expect his name would be before the convention—a surprise equal to that of those upon whom a surprise party calls when they find a table already spread for their entertainment! [Laughter.] Since he is a candidate for a high office, his relations to public questions are proper subjects of examination. Since the speech he made under these embarrassing circumstances has been made the platform of the organization which supports him, it is entitled to a passing notice and review. From the careful collection of extracts from newspapers, &c., with which it abounds, if he had not declared he had been taken entirely by surprise, one would have supposed he had made elaborate preparation. [Laughter.] But there are other cases equally remarkable. A newly-elected Speaker of a Western Legislature, though declaring he was taken by surprise, and unexpectedly called upon, forthwith drew from his pocket and read an elaborate manuscript, returning his thanks for the honor conferred, and apologizing for the imperfections of the address, because he was unaccustomed to extemporaneous speaking. [Great laughter.]

This speech, but for its having been made by Mr. Seymour, in a Convention purified and chastened, and hallowed by the mellow influences of the Ninth-Resolution patriots of last year, might have been taken for a spurious epitome of the works of Oily Gammon. It commences with the declaration that he had uniformly expressed his unwillingness to be a candidate, but, yielding to precedent, while

"Whispering, 'I will ne'er consent'—consented;"

not merely in regard to partial friends, but more because he is impelled to suffer moral martyrdom for the country's good! There has not been before such a forcing process since the rape of the Sabine, and the sacking of Ismal. [Great laughter.] It is true that Mr. Seymour began to decline early, and I mentioned the circumstance to friends six months since, as conclusive evidence that he expected to be a candidate. [Laughter.] I learned years ago that when he began to decline openly, he was on the scent of a nomination. [Laughter.] I cannot of course be expected to speak of the inconsolable grief the partial friends would have experienced if he had persistently and perseveringly declined, but so far as the country is concerned, as Mr. Weller, senior, would have said, I think it would have "managed to surwive," if he had not been forced to an acceptance. It is not probable, however, that the self-sacrifice will be serious, or that the nomination will occasion him any permanent inconvenience beyond the casualties of the race, for the popular mind will do much in his case to relieve uncertainties, to diminish friction, and thereby save the necessity of extensive repairs. It is by no means unlikely that the loyal masses desire him to *run*, but they doubtless would prefer that he should again enter the track to which he is accustomed, on the Wisconsin course, where he could do little harm, instead of running for the executive chair of the Empire State, as the representative of questionable patriotism. [Laughter.]

He eulogizes the convocation of political schemers, of which he was one, and bemoans that compromises were not seasonably offered the South, when all know, and none better than he, that such compromises were offered and urged, and were defeated only because a portion of Southern members engaged in the treasonable conspiracy of disunion, but without courage to vote against them, withdrew, to avoid a vote upon them, and others, by preconcerted arrangement, remained and voted against them, with those known to be opposed to all compromise, and thus secured their defeat.

He shows us that he has been an experienced traveler, scarcely less than the renowned Mungo Park. Though it seems not to have occurred to him, in the hurry of his address, to give us the result of his wanderings and researches, it is notorious that while he may not have found the source of the Nile or the mouth of the Niger in the East, he knows all the crooks and turns in the Fox River, in Wisconsin—a name not unsuited to the occasion of his visit to the West. [Loud laughter.] He permits us to know that he visited Washington, doubtless after his long run in the West, and that he went to the camp of the soldiers, who must have been gratified at his safe return, especially the Wisconsin volunteers, who could inquire for their friends; that there he, naturally enough, found sick and bleeding and languishing men, but I venture he found no runaways, no political schemers or balance-masters—no apologists for the Rebellion of the whole or the half-blood, and none who spend their time in denouncing the Government for prosecuting what is termed an unconstitutional war against conspiracy, treason, rebellion, robbery, piracy, and murder. From thence he was pleased to visit the Capitol, and in language rivaling the hifalutins of the Milford Bard at Balbec and Palmyra, he describes that he traversed the mosaic pavements and gazed upon the ceilings (which no sensible man can look at without condemning the execrable taste of the architect), and was impressed with the strange contrast between its elaborate finish (of Italian gingerbread) and the rude structure of the camp; and being sentimentally inclined, it is not unlikely, in comparing it with the broad prairies of the West, which he had so recently seen, he involuntarily exclaimed with Byron—

"God made the country and man made the town."

But his perseverance did not terminate here. He visited the Congressional Halls, where it is evident he did not aspire to a seat, or he would long before this have declined it. He listened to the stirring debates, the strife and conflicts of which contrasted so strangely with the quiet of the "woods and wilds" to which he had become accustomed, that he was filled, with apprehension and alarm, and he prescribes remedies. The whole burden of his speech is to that end, and to prove the justice and necessity of party organization. He condemns the party action of the Republicans, and then proposes to cure the action of one party by the action of another, upon the true homeopathic principle—*similia similibus curanter.* He serves up to the public a rehash of newspaper criticisms upon the conduct of the war, with their exposures of disgraceful peculation, as though these arguments proved the propriety of substituting politics for patriotism—the separate action of a part for the united action of the whole—a party for the people. He rattles the dry bones of taxation to frighten the masses from their purpose, and faintly whispers repudiation to alarm the public creditor. [Continued laughter.]

Mistakes, errors, blunders, and miscalculations are, in a greater or less degree, inseparable from the conducting of an extensive military campaign, and plunderers are as sure accompaniments of war as vultures are of the battle-field. Would to God we had only those who plundered our material elements, and not those, too, who betray us to death and crucifixion with a kiss! But the remedy consists in increased and not in diminished patriotism—in drawing the honest masses together in a more perfect Union, regardless of political distinctions, and not by dividing them into sections and parties, under the lead of political lazaroni, and attempting to revive decaying organizations with all the bigoted prejudices and hereditary hates, serving to build up corrupt cliques and reward rotten leaders. If incompetency and inefficiency can be corrected, it can be done more effectually by the *whole* than by a *part.* All loyal men are alike interested in putting down rebellion, or in employing the best agencies for that purpose, and why should they not act together? All loyal organizations are, or should be, alike engaged in vindicating the Constitution, and in crushing revolt, and why should they not lay aside for this awful crisis their internal strifes and struggles, and act in one grand and common concert, until the great citadel which protects and shelters all is secured from destruction? No party, as such, is adequate to a work of such magnitude, nor should any one attempt it. The Republican party, for which I claim no right to speak, which is not responsible for me, nor I for it, so far as I understand its position, does not profess to act against the Rebellion as a party, but in theory and in practice lays aside for the occasion, as it did last year, its distinctive action as a party, and its members unite, in common with all loyal Democrats and others who are so disposed, upon a platform inculcating no party ends, but pledges its votaries to the vigilant and thorough prosecution of the war, until Rebellion shall be conquered, and the Constitution acknowledged, without reservation or condition, leaving to every one his full, perfect, and independent political opinions, unaffected or untouched by his associations. To this platform I entirely agree. I despise mere names at any time, and especially at such a time as this. I defy and scorn all ringing of party gongs to gather the hungry and alarm the timid. I act and propose to act entirely independent of party. I desire to put down the Rebellion by force of arms, and until that is done shall act with those who wish to attain that end by the most direct means.

This Union movement is popular and not partisan. It commends itself to every loyal citizen, and not to a part, and all loyal men should enter into it heart and soul. It has not, in all respects, been conducted as I think it should have been at all times, but is nevertheless preferable to party action. Nor is there any party in the field pretending to act as such, except the ravelings and selvedge of all former parties who have taken the honored Democratic name, and under leaders cheating by false pretences, acting from a prejudice too strong for their discernment or moral sentiments, from a party attachment which clings to names and traditions above principles or things, a mistaken comprehension of the questions at issue, or last, though not least, a disloyal heart, and thus enter the field and create division, and aid and encourage Rebellion. This combination seems determined to run its worn-out and creaking machinery amid the blood and carnage, and death-groans of this terrible war, as the last and worst of the Cæsars fiddled while Rome was encircled in flames.

The Democratic party, forsooth! A knot of men with some stray accidental honest elements; with here and there an honest Democrat who supposes this is a war with Abolition almanacs; with leaders composed of Freesoilers and Abolitionists of 1848; chronic fossilized Whigs of 1844 looking for a recharter of a United States Bank; crippled Democrats who have been carried for life in the ambulances of the party; straggling Know-Nothings not inaptly named; Hards so hard that they cracked in seasoning; Softs and Shysters of all shades and periods, and the Ninth-Resolution men of 1861 who proposed to poultice the Rebellion to death by propositions of peace, are now the Democratic party which is to save the country! "What can you expect of a people," said a philosopher, "when a monkey is their God!" Shade of Jefferson, where hast thou flown? Spirit of Jackson! I almost hear you exclaim "By the Eternal!" Mr. Seymour, speaking apparently ex-cathedra, informs the people what this faction, the self-styled Democratic party, proposes to do. The burden of the song is, that they propose to restore the Constitution and obey all Constitutional authority and defend the liberty of speech, and he launches into a homily about observances of law, and invokes the names of early and eminent jurists, as though it had some possible relation to the question, when it has no more application than the farewell address of John Rogers to his children. [Laughter.] This Rebellion cannot well be sued by summons and complaint, nor brought to trial before a justice of the peace or referees under the code, nor silenced by a grand jury, nor be conquered at the County Court, nor held to bail by a judge, nor tried at the circuit, nor have an effectual sentence or judgment affirmed by the Supreme Court or Court of Appeals. No one should fail to sympathize with a candidate, unexpectedly aspiring to gubernatorial honors, whose condition is so necessitous that he cites the words of Lord Mansfield on the occasion of the Gordon or "no Popery" riots nearly a century since, to prove that a Government, assailed by conspiracy and armed Rebellion, has no remedy but what is specified in the Constitution, written in statutes, or prescribed by the slow and ineffectual process of the common law, or if it has, should not employ it, for it means that, or it has no meaning. Here it is:

"When England was agitated by the throes of violence—when the person of the king was insulted; when Parliament was besieged by mobs maddened by bigotry; when the life of Lord Mansfield was sought by infuriated fanatics, and his house burned by incendiary fires, then he uttered those words which checked at once unlawful power and lawless violence. He declared that every citizen was entitled to his rights according to the known procedures of the land. He showed to the world the calm and awful majesty of the law unshaken amid convulsions. Self-reliant in its strength and purity, it was driven to no acts which destroy the spirit of law. Violence was rebuked, the heart of the nation was reassured, a sense of security grew up, and the storm was stilled. Listen to his word:

"'Miserable is the condition of individuals, dangerous is the condition of the State, where there is no certain law, or, what is the same thing, no certain administration of law, by which individuals may be protected, and the State made secure.'"

It is easy to indulge in rhapsodies over or to sentimentalize on the beauties of the common law, and such efforts appear well enough in juvenile law schools, or with beginners at the bar; but when invoked as a means of conquering such a rebellion, they are as ridiculous as would be a homily on moonshine to arrest an earthquake [laughter], an apostrophe to the dews of evening amidst a hurricane [continued laughter], or a prescription of Mrs. Winslow's soothing syrup for the Asiatic Cholera. [Great laughter.] If Mr. Seymour himself had read, or had permitted his hearers to have read from his erudite production a little deeper into this scrap of history, it would have appeared that it was a mere riot or mob, over the repeal of the penal laws against Catholics—a question concerning a particular measure under the Government—and had no relation whatever to the question of the British Government, or its integrity, or its fundamental laws; that Lord Mansfield was one of the victims of violence, and uttered what was excellent sense for the occasion, but which, if it had been proposed as an antidote for a rebellion with half a million of men in arms against the Government, with the avowed intent of subverting it, would have appeared as cheap, and puerile, and shallow, and pedantic then, as its suggestion for the same purpose does now. Our Constitution and written laws are the emanations of Government, prescribing rules and regulations for its ordinary administration and guidance, and defining and limiting its powers for the protection of its citizens. But Governments make Constitutions and laws—Constitutions and laws do not make Governments. [Cheers.] Constitutions and laws are to be observed in all its civil polity, and ordinary exigencies, even in war; but among the first rites and privileges and highest and holiest duties and obligations of Government is the preservation of its own existence. Constitution, law, freedom of speech, liberty of the press—usurpation, tyranny, &c., are words easily prated, and even parrots can be taught them. But men should know that the instincts of a Government, as of an individual when assaulted, are self-defence. The father and protector of a dependent family who should fail to employ all his energies when assailed by a murderer or bandit, and instead thereof proceed to recite from a law book, would, if slain, rank with suicides in the sight of God and man; and a Chief Magistrate who should fail to protect his Government against foreign or domestic foes, armed or unarmed—whether avowed or silent—whether wielding openly the implements of death or insidiously acting as the advocate and apologist of rebellion—would himself be guilty of treason, and would deserve impeachment, conviction and execution. [Great applause.] Those who volunteer as exponents or oracles of constitutions and laws should at least understand the subject they are discussing—should know that in times of peril to the nation martial law inheres in the very essence and existence of every Government as a great necessity, and may be, and should be, asserted when requisite for the preservation of its life and being. A war of rebellion is a fearful and alarming reality, and is neither to be run away from nor quieted by reciting boarding-school homilies. It demands and should receive every element of power which slumbers in the bosom of the nation. When Lord Wellington, upon an exigency proclaimed martial law, on being asked what it was, replied that it was the *discrètion of the Commanding General.* [Cheers.] Military law is the law for the government of the military forces of a nation. Martial law is more rigorous still, wider in its application, and is defined by Smith, an early and eminent writer, in his "English Republic," and by others who have compiled its best definitions, as follows:

"Martial law is the law of war, that depends on the just but arbitrary power of the King. For though he doth not make any laws but by common consent in Parliament, yet, in time of war, by reason of the necessity of it, to guard against dangers that often arise, he useth absolute power, so that his word is law. When, in time of extreme peril to the State, either from *without or within*, the general safety cannot be trusted to the ordinary administration, or the public welfare demands the adoption or execution of extraordinary measures, it may become necessary to declare the existence of martial law."

The President has no such power as a civil magistrate in the ordinary administration of the Government, but, in a time of conspiracy, rebellion, and war, as Commander-in-Chief, when in his judgment the public safety demands it, he possesses, and may and should exert if necessary, as much power as the autocrat of all the Russias, for the purpose of preserving from destruction the Government confided to him. [Great cheering.] It is a power dangerous and liable to abuse—should always be exercised with caution, and only in times of danger; but in such a period it is the Government's salvation and rock of defence. [Cheers.]

The course of the President in arresting spies and the apologists of rebellion—in suppressing treasonable presses—in suspending the habeas corpus, and in laying his hand upon the aiders and comforters and abettors of treason and conspiracy, entitles him to the admiration and thanks of every good citizen. Let assassins whet their knives—let spies and traitors and pimps and informers scowl and gibber and whisper discontent because the "freedom of speech" is abridged—let conspiracy and treason plot at their infernal conferences—let politicians scheme and elongate and contract their gum-elastic platforms to suit emergencies—let trimming, balancing Joseph Surface candidates indulge in ground and lofty tumbling to divert popular attention from the true issue—let pestilent newspapers, engaged in stimulating rebellion and sowing broadcast seeds of disunion and revolt among the people, in the name of the "liberty of the press," spread abroad their ill-concealed hatred of the Government of their fathers, because it fails to minister to their depraved wishes; and when all this has been done, the action of the President in these measures, though probably not free from mistakes and errors, will be approved by honest men and in the sight of Heaven, and will, when rebellion shall only be remembered for the blood it has shed and the wrongs it has perpetrated, "stand the test of talents and of time." Loyal men find the rule no inconvenience. That the disloyal should condemn it, and hate it as they fear it, is natural; for

"No rogue e'er felt the halter draw,
With good opinion of the law."

[Loud laughter.]

Mr. Seymour's claim to speak for the Democratic party, is both spurious and impudent. [Laughter.] He no more represents its men or its masses or its principles in his present course, than Jo. Smith represented the Christian Church. [Roars of laughter.] The old Jacksonian Democracy, when organized upon its true faith, holds, and always has held, the State of New York by a large majority. [Cheers.] The scheming faction of which Mr. Seymour is the nominee and representative, years since debauched, broke up and destroyed the Democratic party by contact with it. Last year it changed its platform four times to get it in good cheating shape [loud laughter], and was then beaten by more than a hundred thousand votes. [Cheers.] This year it hopes to gain strength in the city. Trade is reviving, and Tammany and Mozart, upon those elevated notions of Democratic principles which have long distinguished them, are endeavoring to drive a bargain to divide the offices. It is a proud exhibition before this country and the world just now, and will be successful if it can be determined which should take the *odd trick.* [Laughter.]

The masses of the Democratic party are not now politically organized, but its members are always loyal, and when organized, the party is as true as was its great leader, Jackson. Its members swell the ranks of our brave armies in guarding the Nation's Capital, in protecting that dear symbol of liberty and hope, the Stars and Stripes, from desecration, and in defending the Constitution and the Union. [Cheers.] They are acting with the Union organization at home, and are endeavoring to exhibit to rebellion and to the world, the sublime moral spectacle of a whole people, laying aside political partisan opinions and discussions, and acting together to preserve their revolutionary inheritance from destruction. The members of the narrow, trading, tricky faction, who now strut—the self-constituted heroes of the Democratic party, a name they have learned to mouth better than they have to practice its principles—were nine out of ten against it in the days of its organized action, or if with it, were its mendicants, office-seekers and camp-followers. The true Democrat has no fear that he shall be forever lost, if he acts in common with political opponents in subduing rebellion. He believes he can find himself when the war is over. The spurious one, naturally enough, is fearful if he once gets mingled with Republicans, he will never know himself again, and hence his necessity for keeping up party organization. But even bastard Democrats can be preserved from final loss with a little care. Let them be chalked as farmers chalk sheep when they put lots together which they may wish to separate again, marking the black with white chalk and the white with red. Or write on them as the Dutchman did on his picture of a bear, when he feared the outline of bruin might not be recognized, "*dis ish von bear.*" [Laughter and cheers.]

I will not presume to say what the true Democratic party will do when peace is restored and it is reorganized; but I am at least an older soldier in its ranks than Mr. Seymour ["That's so" —cheers], have longer adhered to its principles and usages, and have as good right to speak for it as he has; and I may, perhaps, with propriety predict what it will not do. That it will not attempt to conquer a nefarious rebellion in arms by propositions of peace; that it will not, by every indirect means of assault upon the Government and apology for Rebellion, afford aid and comfort and encouragement to an armed enemy, tugging at the very heart-strings of the Republic; that it will not organize a factious political party of grinding, growling grumblers to war upon the Government, to embarrass its efforts, to predict its failure, and to exhibit to the enemy a people divided at home, and exhausting themselves in domestic strife; that it will not proclaim Slavery paramount to the Union of our fathers, and delare that if one must go down it should be the Union and not Slavery; that it will exhibit no limping, hesitating, half-and-half fidelity to the Government; no fifth-rib loyalty, inquiring for the health, with a dagger under its garment. [Great cheering.] But, when it acts, its whole course will be direct, sincere, and honorable, upward and onward, and all its energies and efforts will be directed and devoted to the preservation of the land our fathers loved, swearing upon their country's altar, "By the Eternal, the Union must and shall be preserved." [Applause.] A life-long Democrat, I do not hesitate to declare responsibly that the organized action of this knot of politicians, as a spurious Democratic party in this State, has done and is now doing more to encourage the endurance and perseverance of this rebellion, than all the sympathies of England and France combined, and that such is the public judgment—more than all the vessels which have run the blockade together. [Cheers.] The South knew the old Democratic party of this State as a party of power and influence. They hope and believe this faction is its successor, and possesses some of its elements and influences, and await its triumph. Could the murderous tatterdemalions of rebellion, who are described as reeking with a rank compound of villainous smells, shaggy with shreds of what was clothing, and creeping with vermin, attend our polls, they would give this ticket a unanimous vote. [Great laughter.] Could it succeed, Jefferson Davis would proclaim another day of thanksgiving, though it might have to be kept in fasting [laughter and applause], and illuminate Richmond; and well he might, for its success would be more hurtful to the cause of the Union than the loss of the army of the Potomac and the capture and the sacking of Washington. [Cheers.] It is a ticket upon which all the opponents of the war will combine, at home and abroad, and to which they look for relief from their position. Could that illustrious, historic patriot of a neighboring State, who recently started upon the Wisconsin route to *shift* himself into Canada in woman's clothes, to avoid a draft, be permitted, as he should be, to stump New York for this ticket, he would doubtless raise a *hoop* that would silence the most distinguished brave ever produced by Tammany. [Great laughter.]

I have no new light upon the subject of this Rebellion, or the manner in which it should be treated. I stand to-day where I stood when Sumter fell—[cheers]—determined to see my Country's Flag vindicated—to see the supremacy of the Constitution established and upheld—to see sovereign law acknowledged—to see Rebellion crushed—to act with those, and those only, who would go all lengths to break it down—to act against all who would be its defenders or apologists—to act with those who, in pursuing Rebellion, would stop only at the outposts of civilization and Christianity in efforts to destroy it [applause]—to employ every means, moral and material, known to man to cut it up and to cut it down the most effectually, and at the earliest moment. [Great cheering.] I devoted seven of the best years of my life in efforts for the settlement of this accursed question peaceably—that it might be taken out of the political field North and South, and be let alone to work out its own peculiar problem under the mysterious dispensation of a guiding and beneficent Providence. Now that it is unnecessarily made the pretext for a wicked and causeless rebellion by the Southern people, I care not how soon I see its end. [Great cheering and waving of handkerchiefs. "Them's my sentiments."] With no abolition proclivities, in a political sense, but the reverse, I would not have gone out of my way to look upon slavery in this conflict, or to avoid slavery, but would have treated it like any other element, taking it when it would give us strength or weaken them, and employed it accordingly. I have never seen a moment since the outbreak when I would have touched the institution for itself alone, nor when I would not have cut it from its moorings in one hour, if it would have aided in disposing of the rebellion, and I would do the same now. [Applause.] I hold the war power broad enough to cover the whole question, and I confess, in a time when our Government is trembling in the balance before the world, I like to see it exercised when it is well, and boldly, and thoroughly done. [Great applause.]

Let those who take the sword perish with the sword, is my doctrine, and let those who raise a rebellious army against the Constitution, take just such aid and comfort as martial law and the war power in their utmost rigor mete out to them, whether it be hemp, or steel, or lead, or a confiscation of property. If slaves are property, they are subject to the same rules as other property, and should be treated accordingly. There is no charm upon the subject, and should be no mystification over it. I early saw that rebellion, if long continued, would end in emancipation—that from a necessity emancipation was to enter into the question, for as the rebellion progressed and declined, and was on its last legs, it would at the last moment liberate the slaves in its desperation, if events had not sooner practically done so, or emancipation had not then been proclaimed by the Federal Government. I would have preferred practical and real acts in the premises as occasions demanded, under martial law as such, to theories or paper proclamations, for I hold the war power abundant and legislation unnecessary; but the President having determined upon a Proclamation, I would have preferred to see how it would work in the last few months of the old year, to the first day of the new. [Great applause.] But, if the Proclamation weakens rebellion and strengthens Government—as I hope and believe it will—I am for it and all its consequences, and any and every other measure which will conduce to that end The institution has been overworked, and can no longer form political capital on either side, of which politicians of both shades will please take notice. It is to pass away during the present struggle, especially if long continued, and as an element of mischief and disturbance, and as a just retribution to those who have taken up arms against the Government in its name for vile political ends, it has my permission to start at the earliest moment possible, and to make the exodus a complete one. One such Government is worth all the slavery that has existed since Joseph was sold into Egypt.—[Cheers.] If rebellion wishes to avoid these results, and to invoke the Constitution, let it acknowledge its supremacy, embrace tho olive-branch extended by the President, and lay down its arms and close its work of treason and murder. The cry that released contrabands are coming North, is for political effect, and to secure votes from alarmed laborers. When slavery is no longer recognized in the Southern States, the colored race will not struggle for the cold North to compete with our laborers, but those now with us will seek a more congenial clime in the sunny South, where the climate is more agreeable, and the labor and productions better suited to their wants, and tastes, and habits.

The question of candidates, so far as it concerns men, merely, is comparatively of little consequence. The principles they represent are now of the highest possible moment. The Union candidate for Governor, Gen. Wadsworth, I have known for many years. I know him as a gentleman of high social position, of sterling integrity, of manly and honorable bearing, of unpretending habits, and simple tastes—a dispenser of bounteous charities to the poor, who has a heart for suffering man, wherever his lot may be cast; who, when Ireland was perishing with famine, sent a cargo of provisions to the relief of her starving children; who discharges all his relations with fidelity. I do not know whether I agree with him in all political opinions, or not, and do not care. I agree with him in the great practical idea of putting down this infernal Rebellion at all hazards, at any cost; and this is the only matter directly under consideration. And I agree with him substantially in his excellent and manly and sensible letter by which he declares his acceptance of the nomination. I believe his election at this time as Chief Magistrate of this great State essential to that end; that his defeat would be disastrous; and shall support him accordingly, as every truly loyal man of every party should do. Let every honest elector, independent of all party names, which are now used only for cheats for the people, and we may pass upon the conduct of these two candidates since the commencement of the rebellion—let them read the noble, out-spoken letter of one, and the cautious, backing and filling speech of the other, and then see who is worthy of support. The intrepid Tremain has already spoken for himself, and will speak again. [Loud applause.] He is a Union Democrat and a representative of the Union sentiment. He may laugh at the assaults and detractions of those who seek to build up a selfish, rotten organization in the name of Democracy, as a capital for spoils and political stock-jobbers. They envy his position and fear him, and hate him, for he early took off their shallow mask and impaled their leader. He has not yet dismissed them, but may be heard from hereafter by all interested, to their entire satisfaction. Mr. Jones, the candidate for Lieutenant-Governor on the bogus ticket, deserves better company and a better fate. If he had kept one, he might have secured the other, and he probably regrets with me that he had not done so. He was put on the ticket by men who have already injured him by their associations past remedy, in the hope of cheating a few true Democrats into the support of the ticket. But this will all fail, and Mr. Jones, like Tray in the fable, will be punished for being in bad company. [Laughter.] The residue of the candidates upon the respective tickets may be said to fairly stand as the representatives of those who placed them in nomination, remembering that Ladue and Willman and Hughes are true men.

The Liquor Dealer's Association, those who distil the very nectar of the gods, those also who can, like a magician, draw half a dozen kinds of wine from the same cask, those whose whiskey will kill further and surer than a rebel musket, patriotically met recently and naturally and suitably nominated Mr. Seymour as their representative. [Laughter.] This was, doubtless, to compensate him for the mental agony and physical suffering he experienced, according to Mr. Delevan, when in labor with a veto against a prohibitory law a few years since, to which he was to set his name. This being done, as the papers inform us, the Dealers' Convention went into liquidation, adjourning in *good spirits*. [Great laughter.] These last two facts are interesting and important. The public will be glad to learn of the adjournment, and their customers that their spirits were good. [Laughter.]

Must not every candid man admit that the whole course of Mr. Seymour, from the breaking out of the rebellion to the present moment, has been destitute of patriotism, or good or generous impulses or emotions? Must not every honest elector admit that he has exhibited only the characteristics of the mere politician, and of a cold, calculating, and trimming one at that?

Must not every honest man declare that the speech-platform upon which he professes to stand is deceitful in its conception and spirit, lacking frankness, manhood, and out-spoken fairness and honesty, but contaminated by an all-over of slipperyness and design—intended to strike a blow at our Government and conceal the hand.

It is idle, my friends, to prosecute this war against rebellion by halves. It is worse than idle to send our sons to the field of blood and leave politicians at home who are denouncing Government, apologizing for rebellion, and ar. inculcating, no matter how stealthily or covertly, cowardly and fatal propositions of peace. Rebellion knows, from spies and sympathizers quite too near us, what is going on in our midst as well as we do. It is struggling on in the hope that this peace party may gain the ascendency, when it expects to be forgiven for its treason, have murder washed from its bloody hands, and be rewarded for its villainy by liberal propositions. This party, with its propositions of peace, having been exposed, abashed, and ingloriously overthrown last year, has covered its framework this, with a veneering of a different shade, but quite too flimsy to deceive a discerning and loyal people. Like the cat in the fable, it has whitewashed its coat, but the teeth and claws are plainly discernible. [Laughter.] Call back your sons, I repeat, or crush this insidious monster at home and the rebellion abroad together. Rebellion has lost faith in expected foreign recognition. Its miserable sympathizers in England lack courage to come to time. Even Disraeli, who O'Connell said was a regular lineal descendant of the hardened thief, fails to meet the occasion as expected. [Laughter.] Its hope now rests in the aid and sympathy it can command in the loyal States, to save it from the condign punishment and ignoble end which awaits it, and looks more to the success of this ticket to-day than to the exploits of Stonewall Jackson. Call back your sons, I say again, or crush this political hope of rebellion at home. When this hideous monster sees us united as one man, in one common purpose to crush it, it will yield; but until then it will struggle on, like the writhings of a venomous serpent, till exterminated. It would long since have yielded, but for hope of propositions of peace from political quarters, and terms of accommodation; and but for seeing the Executive denounced for unconstitutional acts, and a party rising up opposing the war in effect if not in name—for rebel leaders understand the matter in all its bearings.

Alas! how many brave spirits have been quenched forever because of this shameful, sinful division—by reason of this miserable political ambition to raise up a successful party at home to gain office and spoils. But God will bring its actors to judgment. Every household has been bereaved.

> There is no flock, however watched or tended,
> But one dead lamb is there;
> There is no fireside, howsoe'er defended,
> But has one vacant chair.
>
> The air is full of farewells to the dying,
> And mournings for the dead:
> The heart of Rachel, for her children crying,
> Will not be comforted.

Our fair-haired boys periled their lives in endeavoring to crush a rebellion which gains hope, and tenacity, and endurance, and perseverance, in its work of conspiracy and treason and murder, and holds on because it sees a peace-war party rising up stealthily and in disguise among us at home. Their bones are bleaching upon every battle-field in the rebel States. Those who loved them ask you where they are! You cannot raise the dead; but, in the name of Heaven, call back the living that are yet spared to us, or destroy, at one blow, one of the chief hopes of rebellion at home, a political organization, to which rebellion instinctively turns for relief. But yesterday a proud boy in the heyday of life and hope fell. He was the only son of his mother, and she was a widow; he fell by the hand of a rebel murderer, nerved on by the hope that political divisions in the loyal States would give rebellion aid and comfort, and propositions of peace. She asks you with trembling lip and tearful eye for the idol of her heart, her hope and joy. May He who tempers the winds to the shorn lamb protect *her!* You cannot restore her child, but you can destroy one of the accursed causes which protract this bloody and terrible war, the politicians' hope. The storms of autumn beat upon the log-cabin standing by the little brook beyond the hills. The winds moan, and the leaves rustle, and night is gathering. A woman weeps over a hearth cold and cheerless and desolate. A group of little children, with curious, anxious faces, hang upon her knee wondering why she weeps, and are asking for their father.

> "Alas!
> Nor wife, nor children, more shall he behold;
> Nor friends, nor sacred home."

He fills an unknown bloody grave in the land of rebellion, where he marched to aid in preserving the inheritance of his Revolutionary sire. But he was murdered in expectation of propositions of peace from politicians, who fear rebellion will not be constitutionally treated, or in the hope of some new reading of the Constitution which would exempt rebellion from censure and punishment. [Sensation.] That bereaved widow in her destitution looks to you. Those children "demand their sire with tears of artless innocence." You cannot restore him. God alone can shield and comfort the widow and the fatherless. But you can remove one of the chief causes which serves to protract this hellish malignity and mischief at the ballot-box. [Great applause.] You can cancel the demands of hungry politicians. A settler in the far West upon the Indian border has volunteered, with the true spirit of the pioneer, to defend his country's flag. His wife and children are aroused from their slumbers at midnight by the yells of savage hell-hounds, to perish by the tomahawk and scalping-knife; the cabin is in flames, and the ferocious monsters, with hands dripping with the blood of innocence, bear away their trophies to exhibit for reward to more ferocious monsters still—savages professing Christianity —conspirators and rebels, who stimulate the red man to murder defenceless women and children that they may procure from political traders, at an early moment, liberal propositions of peace and compromise. That borderer will return to greet his loved ones, but they are not there. A heap of ashes is all that is left him; tears roll copiously down his sunburnt visage, but, like the fallow-deer, he weeps alone. You cannot bring back to his embrace the beloved object of his affection, but by precept and example you can aid in removing the detestable hope that a political party can succeed, in whole or in part, in sympathy with rebellion. [Sensation.]

Let, then, I say, the people of the loyal States be united—let them act together as one man. Let no political organization, as such, be supported or encouraged or tolerated; but let all lovers of their country and its institutions meet for public action and effort in a common union. Let rebellion in all its protean forms and all its elements be crushed by every hand and cursed by every lip, in its moral or material forces, in the egg or in the serpent, open or disguised, in its full strength or diluted, in the field or in the political canvass, in battles of blood or at the polls, at home or abroad. [Great applause.] This is demanded in the name of Revolutionary memories, in the name of Liberty and the rights of man, in the sacred name of humanity and religion, in the name of fathers whose sons have been slain, of widows whose husbands have been murdered, of mothers who have been bereaved of their children, of children who have been robbed of those to whom Providence taught them to look for protection, of society which mourns the destruction of its members, of the dead whose blood has been shed to preserve our Government from shame, our land from desecration, our homes from the torch—in the name of justice, truth, and peace, and of man's last best hope beneath the skies. Rebellion is doomed; its last hope is in political aid by home divisions. Destroy this hope, and our Government shall never die. [Immense cheering.]

The President then introduced, amid great applause, the Hon. Lyman Tremain, who said:

I thank you sincerely for those enthusiastic cheers. I thank your Chairman for the warm, complimentary, and undeserved eulogium he has bestowed upon me. But in the great crisis through which we are now passing, the individual sinks into insignificance in comparison with the great cause in which he is engaged; and I have not the vanity to suppose that this great demonstration is due to any popularity which I possess. I prefer rather to ascribe it to its true cause, that great and noble cause of which I chance to be a representative and with which I am identified.

On the 24th of September last a Convention was held in a central city of New York, more important than any other political Convention which has ever been convened within the State; for its proceedings were more intimately connected with the life and perpetuity of our Government and our free institutions. This Convention determined, as its principal object, to present a platform and a ticket for the support of the people of the State of New York, which should unmistakably represent two great cardinal principles—the one, the determination of the people of the State of New York, while this terrible rebellion lasts, to ignore all the partisan differences and prejudices of the past, and to recognize the great fact that the civil war that is now raging around us has burst up the cobweb ties of party in the purer blaze of devotion to our country. Another principle which that Convention sought to represent, was the stern, inflexible resolution of the loyal and patriotic State of New York to push forward this war for the preservation of our Government to a successful termination, by infusing into its prosecution, with all their hearts and all their soul and all their strength, the entire vigor, energy, resources, influence, and means of this great and powerful Commonwealth.

This Convention consisted of Republicans, and Democrats, and Americans, and Whigs, and loyal citizens without partisan affinities; and embraced an amount of wealth and worth, of earnestness and respectability, of influence and of patriotism rarely equaled, never surpassed; marked, too, by a most extraordinary absence of anything like rowdyism or intemperance, which constituted a marked feature in its character and its proceedings.

Their attention was first called to the selection of an appropriate principal standard-bearer to lead the loyal masses of this State in this contest. They fortunately found that there was a citizen of New York, of great private worth and personal popularity, whose large property naturally and necessarily made him conservative in all his views and principles and feelings; but more than this, they found that he had given the most unmistakable evidence of that patriotic devotion which was desired; that when this rebellion first broke out, he had abandoned the pleasures and comforts and luxuries of his own fireside, and, with three sons, had entered the field, where, in high military position, he had been assiduously engaged in devoting himself, night and day, to the service of his country. This man was one whose charities were not confined to the limits of his own land; but, in that hour when Ireland was suffering from starvation, out of his own purse and by his own means, he loaded a ship with provisions, which he caused to be sent and distributed among the suffering poor of the Emerald Isle. They found, too, in this person the most unmistakable evidence, in all his public and private acts, that he was devoted, body and soul, faithfully and honestly, to the great work of sustaining the Union in the work of crushing out this unholy rebellion, which threatened its existence. So strongly was the sentiment of the Convention in his favor, that, upon the first ballot, he received about two-thirds of the entire number of ballots; and the selection thus made was immediately confirmed with cheers and an enthusiasm rarely witnessed in a political body. I need not mention to you that the gentleman thus selected was Gen. James S. Wadsworth. [Applause.]

The Convention next turned its attention to the selection of a candidate for the second office in the State; and, true to its principle of ignoring the lines of party—the first candidate being a Republican—they turned their attention for the second office to one who, while party lines existed, had been a Democrat of the straightest sect; with nothing to recommend him to their favorable consideration for that high office to which he was invited to accept the nomination, except that from the time when the rebellion broke out, he had been earnestly and honestly engaged, body and soul, in sustaining the arms of the Government in suppressing it. With a unanimity and enthusiasm such as I have never witnessed before, and which produced an impression that I shall carry gratefully with me to the latest moment of my existence, that Convention conferred the nomination for Lieutenant-Governor upon the individual who stands before you to-night.

And now, Gentlemen, as a part of the august tribunal of the people of the State, before whom the issue now pending is to be brought to trial, and by whom the verdict is to be rendered, you have a right, and I recognize to its fullest extent that right, to know what my sentiments are upon the great and the only absorbing issue that fills all hearts and all minds. Allow me then to state, in a few words, that I am, from the crown of my head to the soles of my feet, perpendicularly, horizontally, and diagonally [laughter], in every emotion of my heart, in every faculty of my mind, and in every pulsation of my heart, an unreserved and unconditional Union War Democrat [prolonged applause], standing upon the platform of "War, war to the knife" [renewed applause]; that so far as I am concerned, neither in thought, word, or deed, shall the idea be harbored that this glorious Union, which God and nature intended to be one and indissoluble, shall ever be divided; inflexibly opposed to the entertaining of any proposition, at any time or under any circumstances, that peace with armed rebels shall be thought of, unless it is a peace upon the solid, permanent, and enduring basis of the unconditional submission of every armed rebel in this glorious land. [Enthusiastic cheering.]

I have observed that this canvass is to be waged by a disregard of all the ordinary civilities, courtesies, decencies, or regard to truth of ordinary political controversies, and that it is to be a war characteristic of the barbarous rebellion and those sympathizing with it at home and abroad. [Cheers.] I hear already at my heels the barking of the whole secession pack, from the well-fed bulldog of the party down through the kennel to "Tray, Blanche, and Sweet-heart," who bark as their masters bid them. I admit that it was an honor to receive in my person the blows that I have received in behalf of that great, patriotic cause with which I stand identified. I counted the cost of breaking away from the ties of that misguided clique who have stolen the livery of Democracy as they would steal the livery of heaven to serve the devil in. [Cheers.] I say I have entered upon this warfare against the enemies of our country whether they are to be found in the Confederate States or the State of New York. I have drawn the sword and thrown away the scabbard and broken down the bridges behind me. [Cheers.] Mr. Tremain went on to say that a political contest at this time and under these circumstances was repugnant to all his tastes and all his feelings. The question arose, who caused it—who forced us into the necessity of a political contest to secure a loyal Government to the State of New York at a time when the country demanded the active services of her every son in directly putting down this atrocious rebellion, and while yet the State lacked 35,000 of having filled her quota of troops under the recent call of the President? The responsibility rested only and exclusively upon those leaders of an organization calling itself Democrat, who had put forth Horatio Seymour as their candidate. [Cheers.] The proofs to sustain that assertion were overwhelming. Mr. Tremain adverted to the offer made by the Republican State Central Committee to the Democratic Committee a year ago to make a common ticket, which was rejected by the Democratic Committee, although it would have secured them half the offices, and a share of the Presidential patronage in the State. He asked, if those gentlemen were in their hearts in favor of the prosecution of this war for the suppression of the rebellion, what earthly reason could have been given for not accepting that generous and magnanimous offer? The Democratic State Committee not only rejected the offer, but refused to let the Democratic masses meet in convention on the same day and in the same place with the Republican Convention, and the consequence was that they were beaten by a hundred thousand majority. Could such a fatal mistake have been committed, had the Democratic party been under the control of the men of 25 years ago, Edwin Croswell, John A. Dix, Silas Wright, Daniel S. Dickinson, or Azariah C. Flagg? [Loud applause.] Was there a man who could doubt that their answer would have been unanimously and unmistakably in favor of accepting the proposition? What, they would have said: Talk about running an organization and calling it Democracy now! Go to the city of Albany in the spring, when the Hudson River is breaking up, and the great masses of ice filling it from bank to bank are crushing everything before them, moving with an irresistible and overwhelming power, and find a man proposing to build a board raft, and comes down on it with his family to the city of New York, and that man is wise compared with you who talk about forming a party when the very fabric of our Government is tottering. [Loud applause.] Mr. Tremain proceeded to say that, being on the Legislative Union Committee this year, he had succeeded in inducing that committee to make another proposition to other organizations, and they had again rejected the offer to bury the hatchet of party for the prosecution of the war. Mr. Seymour insisted upon the wisdom and propriety of maintaining a political organization, and, among other reasons for it, showed it was just the thing the President and the Border States desired, and the Republican party was so destitute of wisdom, not having Horatio and his associates in it, that they could not carry on the Government; that his party alone possessed the capacity and intellect necessary to crush out the rebellion. Now he could demonstrate to the true, loyal Democrats, who had sent their sons and their money to this war, that there was not one single principle for which we contended which had not been an issue with which the old Democratic party, in the days of its power and its glory, had been identified and united; and there was not one single principle contended for by the organization represented by Horatio Seymour, but what was a direct descendent from the principles of the Hartford Convention. The Hartford Convention, too, like Seymour, pretended to be in favor of the war. But the very fact that it was carping at the conduct of the war at a time when every energy of our country should be engaged in prosecuting it, condemned the old Federal party to go down be neath the waves of a popular indignation so deep that no bubble ever rose to tell the spot where they went down. [Loud Cheers.]

He believed that Andrew Jackson was regarded as a pretty good Democrat in his day. But he would not be permitted to sit in the Seymour party. He happened to be on record in regard to just such a rebellion as this. Mr. Tremain read a passage from Jackson's proclamation in 1832, adjuring the citizens of South Carolina to return to obedience to the Constitution, and telling them that they could not be its destroyers. Suppose Andrew Jackson were President now, and Massachusetts, being (for the sake of the supposition) under the control of the Abolitionists, had seceded, and her sisters had gone with her, and a Confederate Government had been established, and Andrew Jackson had undertaken to put it down: did they suppose that a single Democrat would allow any Horatio Seymour to make speeches denouncing him for it by the three column? Why should Democrats be tied to the miserable Secession car now? Thomas Jefferson was a pretty good Democrat, not such an one as Benjamin Wood, but a very good Democrat for all that. He acquired Louisiana, and the nation paid for her, and now that Louisiana claimed to go out; and the pauper States of Florida and Texas, which could not raise money enough to pay the expenses of the United States troops sent down to protect them, claimed to have set up for free and independent States. Stephen A. Douglas was a pretty good Democrat, but he was deprived of his place on Committees in the Senate by the Secession cabal, and the majority of the Democratic Convention was not allowed by them to nominate him. (At this point, as two or three disturbers were very quietly put out by the police.) The old Democracy had always stood ready to crush out anything directed against the foreigners. Where did the two parties stand now in regard to the foreigner? The Union party had put an honorable German, Andreas Willmann, upon their ticket (loud applause), while the Seymour party had formed a coalition with the rump of the Know-Nothing party. (Laughter.) He now understood that their principal reliance was upon the support of the adopted citizens of New York and Albany and Buffalo. What thought adopted citizens? What thought the countrymen of Heintzelman and Sigel?" (Great applause, and "Three cheers for Sigel.") What thought the countrymen of the gallant Corcoran and Meagher? (Loud cheering.) What thought they of this alliance with the ghost of a party whose war-cry had been, when it was alive, "Put none but Americans on guard"? The singular movement called "Anti-Prohibition" party was extraordinarily singular, considering that there was and could be no Prohibitionary law, the principle having been decided to be unconstitutional. Mr. Tremain maintained that Wadsworth was the true conservative. Seymour stood upon a platform whereby he would stand pledged, if elected, to resist by force any attempt of the Federal Government to arrest a traitor in the State of New York. Seymour suggested the repudiation by the State of the United States debt. He said it was very unfortunate that the United States stocks were exempt from taxation, though by that act Congress had placed the credit of the Government above grade, John Bull to the contrary notwithstanding. It might be conservative for him to oppose the Administration, to say that apologies exist for this treason, to hold in terrorem over the Government that this sacred debt of $600,000,-000 should be repudiated; but it sounded very like the conservatism of Jack Cade, whose bountiful promises to his followers when he should be King of England, Mr. Tremain quoted amid great laughter.

Mr. Tremain continued: There is only one other element upon which I would touch; I refer to the recent Proclamation issued by Abraham Lincoln [great applause], that on the 1st of January next the slaves of all Rebel States shall be emancipated forever, and that for citizens who are loyal he will recommend compensation to Congress. Now, in the first place, as to the power of the President. The Constitution declares that the President shall be the Commander-in-Chief of the Army and Navy of the United States, and of the militia of the several States when called into the service of the United State s The power of controlling the entire militia when they are called out by Congress, is vested exclusively in the Chief Magistrate, whom our framers of the Constitution believed would be selected with reference to the responsibility of the trust confided to him. The framers of the Constitution knew that ancient Republics had fallen because the control of the military power had been vested in a senate or in an oligarchy, or in different heads, and they, therefore, framed this provision of the Constitution of which Judge Story says that the powers are obviously of an executive nature. The Supreme Court had passed upon this question. President Polk exercised the power in reference, even to foreign territory; he superseded the civil by the military law in Mexico under which he regulated the payment of duties, and Chief-Justice Taney, in pronouncing upon the legality of that action, said that his power and duty were purely military; as Commander-in-Chief, he was authorized to direct the movements of the military forces placed by law at his command, and to employ them in the manner which he might deem most proper to harass and subdue the enemy. Abraham Lincoln, as the Commander-in-Chief of the Army of the United States, on looking over the whole field, says: After the experience of eighteen months, I find that these slaves of the Rebels are their principal support. I find that by this involuntary servitude they are able to furnish thousands of men to dig their ditches, and do the work which otherwise their white troops would be obliged to do, so keeping them fresh and ready for duty. He says: I find, further, that when all the men from 15 to 55 are pressed into the rebel army, they can leave their slaves at home to do their work. Now here, he says, if there were a great place for the deposit of rifles and muskets, no man could doubt that I could use the whole power of the nation to take it away from them. Ah, but it is urged, the Constitution does not allow it without due process of law. I suppose the President has a right, through the army, to arrest rebels without a warrant issued by a Justice of Peace, or to shoot them down without an indictment, and by the same power, he says, he has the right to say, I will bring the whole military force of this nation against this institution of slavery that sustains and encourages this rebellion. [Loud and long-continued applause and waving of handkerchiefs.] That military order is binding upon every officer and soldier of his army, and I rejoice that the papers of to-day have furnished an order issued by Gen. McClellan, in which he shows that he understands his duties as an officer, and he puts the whole subject in this single paragraph:

> Discussion by officers and the soldiers concerning public measures determined upon and declared by the Government, when carried at all beyond the ordinary temperate and respectful expression of opinion, tend greatly to impair and destroy the discipline and efficiency of troops, by substituting the spirit of political faction for that firm, steady and earnest support of the authority of the Government, which is the highest duty of the American Soldier.

[Loud applause.]

Gen. Wadsworth hits the nail on the head in this language in his letter of acceptance:

> Nor is the question now before us one of philanthropy alone, sacred as are the principles therein involved nor is it a question of abstract ideas, involving an unprofitable discussion of the equality of races. It is simply a question of war, of national life or death, and of the mode in which we can most surely and effectually uphold our Government and maintain its unity and supremacy.

Now the position of the Government is substantially this: It says this lion of slavery has come out from its Constitutional intrenchments, and it has leaped at the throat of the Government, and endeavored to take its life. He has been driven back into his jungle, and now we propose to take his lordship by the mane,

> And damned be he who first cries Hold!
> Enough!

It is not a question of original abolition. If it had been, the President would not have waited eighteen months; he would not have recognized the attribute in loyal States. He has been forced forward step by step, until he has determined to take this monster slavery by the throat. [Great applause.] I think I can see the dawning of a brighter day. General Jackson once got into a life and death struggle with the great moneyed power of this country, and people who were cowardly and timid talked some as they do now. Andrew Jackson said: It must be crushed, and the great cities shrugged their shoulders and abandoned the old man, but he appealed to the great patriotic heart of the country, and he found, as Abraham Lincoln will find now, Tom Bentons standing up everywhere to support him. And now Abraham Lincoln appeals for his support to the loyal people of the State of New York, and the question is, shall he be sustained? [Cheers, "Yes, yes!"] Every officer and soldier in the army is bound to acquiesce. Where should Horatio Seymour stand? He must show his hand. Is he for or against the proclamation? He who stirs up the sentiments of the people against the lawful order of the Commander-in-chief is guilty of sedition. [Cheers, cries of "That's it."] There is one particular distinction between the conduct of the Union men and that of the Seymourites. Whenever we meet, we remember our brothers and sons in the army; no such word of encouragement has gone out from any Seymourite meeting in the State. And I desire again to call upon you to show your sympathies for those noble-hearted men who have gone forth periling their lives for us and our children, and to do full justice to that youthful commander, General McClellan. [Applause.] Let not the reputation of that brave, and scientific, and skillful commander be damaged because sympathizers with the rebellion have attempted the unholy work of appropriating him to themselves. And I ask you to send up three cheers; which shall be echoed by the Army of the Potomac. Give three cheers for our army, embracing every officer and soldier in it, from General McClellan down to the humblest private in the ranks.

[Three times three were given, followed by three cheers for Lyman Tremain, and earnest voices shouted, "God bless Abraham Lincoln!"]

SPEECH OF GEN. JAMES S. WADSWORTH.

Gen. WADSWORTH was serenaded at Washington on Saturday evening, when a great crowd of New York and other hearty Unionists were present. Being asked to respond to the acclamations of his many friends, Gen. WADSWORTH spoke as follows:

I thank you, gentlemen, for the honor you do me in making this visit. I suppose I may assume that you come to congratulate me upon having received from the Convention of the State of New York—a Convention composed of the truest friends of this Government, the truest friends of the country, and the most earnest supporters of the war—on having received from that Convention the nomination to the distinguished position of Governor of the State of New York. While I cannot allow myself to over-estimate the compliment of this nomination; while I cannot allow myself to misunderstand it, or to receive it in any considerable degree as a personal compliment, I need not say how highly I appreciate it. I have not earned it, gentlemen, by any public service of my own in my native State. I have never held any public position, or any official position there. I am known only as a citizen who has pursued his avocations during most of his life entirely in the privacy of home. But the gentlemen who have brought forward my name have done so largely on trust. While I cannot claim that this nomination is the result of any services which I have rendered, or is a reward for any merit in me, I do claim for it significance and meaning plainly marked. I have been brought forward, gentlemen, by men who are in earnest, and they brought me forward because they believed that I was in earnest. (Cries of "Good," and cheers.) These men believe that this rebellion can be crushed, that it ought to be crushed, and they intend that it shall be crushed. (Applause.) They intend to uphold this noble Republican Government of ours. They intend to hold together this country, hold it together at whatever cost of life, of blood, of suffering, of treasure. At whatever cost, they intend to hold it together—to make it desolate, devastated, if need be, but to hold it together, one country, and that a free country—("Good," and cheers)—a land of refuge, as it has been in days past, for the oppressed from all parts of the world. They have brought me forward, gentlemen, as their standard-bearer, because I believe what they believe, I think what they think, I feel as they feel, on these great questions. They do not wish, they do not intend, to survive the dismemberment of their country, and they do not believe that I wish to survive it, or that my children should survive it. (Cheers.) These are the thoughts which have influenced them in bringing me forward, and I trust that in that light, however poor as may be my claim in other respects, I shall receive the approbation and support of the sons of New York who may be here. (Cries, "You will.")

I do not propose, gentlemen, on this occasion—it would be obviously improper in me, in the position which I now occupy—to enter at large into a discussion of the conduct of the war, or the policy of the Government. Sufficient for us to know, gentlemen, that the Government has given us the most solemn and repeated assurances—and it is sustained by the public sentiment of the loyal people who gather to its support—that the war will be prosecuted with the utmost military energy, and that all the means, agencies, and appliances of honorable war will be availed of to carry it on and bring this struggle to an end. It would have been criminal folly in the Government to have overlooked one great element of Southern society—an element which may be, and will be, according as we use it—an element of weakness or an element of strength. It would have been criminal folly in the Government to have overlooked or forgotten the fact that we are fighting against an aristocracy, base and selfish, but still a powerful aristocracy; and it would have been worse than folly to suppose that they could put down the Rebellion and save the aristocracy. A year and a half of bitter experience has proved to us that we cannot do that—that we shall fail if we attempt such a thing, and fail ignobly. We have moistened a hundred battle-fields with the blood of our sons. We are surrounded with hospitals, with the sick and suffering, with wounded and dying men. Almost every household in the North is filled with gloom and weeping for some beloved member, who has gone forth to return no more; and what have we gained? Is it enough that we are safe on this side of the Potomac? Are we repaid for all our sacrifices by this consolation? I think not. And yet, gentlemen, what has this powerful aristocracy done for us that it is entitled to our sympathy? What has it done with this Government, but use it for its own aggrandizement, and failing in that, rise up to overthrow it? I have never failed, gentlemen, previous to the outbreak of this Rebellion, in any public and proper occasion, to declare my earnest devotion to the Constitution of the United States, and my desire to uphold it, with what are called its compromises and concessions in behalf of Slavery.

But, gentlemen, Secession and War, bloody and relentless war, have changed our relations to that which is the cause and the source of the war. (Applause, and cries of "That's it.") We have the right, we are bound moreover by the most solemn obligations of duty, to use this agency, so far as we can, to put an end to this struggle, and to save the lives of white men who are perishing by thousands in this country. How long are we to bear the insolence of this Southern aristocracy? Have we not borne it long enough? Has it not long enough disturbed and distracted our counsels, and paralyzed our energies? Has it not long enough paralyzed the energies of the country? Nay, more, has it not long enough, in the eyes of the other civilized nations of the world, covered us with infamy? (A Voice—It has even so.) But, be that as it may, the issue is made up, and we must conquer it or be conquered by it. This struggle is already far advanced—it is near its end. We are in the pangs of dissolution, or we are in the pangs of exorcism. If we would save ourselves, we must cast out the devil which has tormented and disgraced us from the hour of our national birth. ("Good, good.") We want peace; but more than we want peace, we want a country. We want peace, but we want an honorable peace, a permanent peace, a solid peace. When we have achieved that, we shall commence on a career of prosperity such as we have never known, and such as the world has never before witnessed. We shall spring up at one bound to be the mightiest and the freest and the happiest people on the face of the earth. (Cheers.) I thank you, gentlemen, for the patience with which you have listened to me. (Prolonged, enthusiastic cheering.)

GEN. WADSWORTH'S LETTER OF ACCEPTANCE.

LETTER OF THE PRESIDENT OF THE CONVENTION.

New York, Sept. 29, 1862.

GEN. JAMES S. WADSWORTH.

Dear Sir—I have the honor to inform you that you were nominated for the office of Governor of the State of New York, by a Convention composed of men resolved to maintain the integrity of the Union without regard to their past party relations, and held at Syracuse, on the 24th of the present month.

I enclose the series of resolutions adopted by the Convention, as an indication of its sentiments and purposes.

Your nomination was made with a very remarkable degree of unanimity and enthusiasm, and, on behalf of the Convention, I beg leave respectfully to request your acceptance of it.

I am, very respectfully,
Your obedient servant,
HENRY J. RAYMOND.
President of the Convention.

GEN. WADSWORTH'S REPLY.

Washington, Oct. 2, 1862.

HON. HENRY J. RAYMOND,
President, &c.

Dear Sir—I have the pleasure to acknowledge the receipt of your letter of Sept. 29, informing me that the Convention held at Syracuse on the 24th of that month, composed of men resolved to maintain the integrity of the Union, irrespective of their previous party associations, had done me the honor of placing my name before the electors of the State of New York for the office of Governor.

I respectfully accept the nomination.

I cordially agree with the Convention in the sentiments expressed in their resolutions, and, if elected, I shall zealously labor to carry out their wishes as therein defined.

I might, perhaps, with propriety, stop here; but as the duties of my present position will not allow me to return to New York for some time, and possibly not until after the election has been held, I ask your indulgence while I express briefly my views as to the questions involved in the canvass.

I think I cannot be mistaken in assuming that the election will turn upon the necessity of sustaining our National Government in its efforts to uphold itself, and maintain its territorial integrity, and especially upon the Proclamation of the President, issued to that end, and referred to in the fourth resolution of the Convention.

I entirely approve of that Proclamation, and commend it to the support of the electors of New York, for the following reasons:

1. It is an effectual aid to the speedy and complete suppression of the rebellion.

Six or eight millions of whites, having had time to organize their government, and arm their troops, fed and supported by the labor of four millions of slaves, present the most formidable rebellion recorded in history.

Strike from this rebellion the support which it derives from the unrequited toil of these slaves, and its foundation will be undermined.

2. It is the most humane method of putting down the rebellion, the history of which has clearly proved that the fears of slave insurrections and massacres are entirely unfounded. While the slaves earnestly desire freedom, they have shown no disposition to injure their masters. They will cease to work for them without wages, but they will form, throughout the Southern States, the most peaceful and docile peasantry on the face of the earth.

The Slaveowners once compelled to labor for their own support, the war must cease, and its appalling carnage come to an end.

3. The emancipation once effected, the Northern States would be forever relieved, as it is right that they should be, from the fears of a great influx of African laborers, disturbing the relations of those Northern industrial classes who have so freely given their lives to the support of the Government.

This done, and the whole African population will drift to the South, where it will find a congenial climate and vast tracts of land never yet cultivated.

I forbear to enter into the discussion of the great increase of trade to the Northern States and the whole commercial world, which would result from the wants of four millions of free and paid laborers over the same number held as heretofore in Slavery.

I forbear, also, to enter into the question of the ultimate vast increase in the production of the great Southern staples. This is not a time to consider questions of profit. It will long be remembered, to the great honor of the merchants, bankers, and manufacturers of the North, that giving the lie to the calumnies of slave-breeding aristocrats, who charge them with being degraded and controlled by the petty profits of traffic, they have met the numerous sacrifices of this great struggle with a cheerfulness and promptness of which history furnishes no parallel.

Nor is the question now before us one of philanthropy alone, sacred as are the principles therein involved; nor is it a question of abstract ideas, involving an unprofitable discussion of the equality of races. It is simply a question of war, of National life or death, and of the mode in which we can most surely and effectually uphold our Government and maintain its unity and supremacy.

Our foreign enemies, for it is not to be disguised that we have such, reproach us with waging a territorial war. So we do, but that territory is *our country.* For maintaining its greatness and power among the nations of the earth, by holding it together, they hate us. We can bear that; but if we were to yield to their suggestions, and submit to its dismemberment, they would forever despise us.

This great domain, from the Lakes to the Gulf, from the Atlantic to the Pacific, one country; governed by one idea—freedom—is yet destined to dictate terms, if need be, to the world in arms, and I hold that man to be a traitor and a coward, who, under any defeats, any pressure of adversity however great, any calamities however dire, would give up one acre of it.

It is more than a year since I left our State. Great changes have taken place within that period. Costly victories and disastrous defeats have, in the vicissitudes of war, befallen our arms. Bereavements and destitution have overtaken many families.

I can only judge of the spirit of my fellow-citizens of New York, by that of her gallant sons who have rushed to the field. These I have seen in great numbers, and particularly those who have been in the hospitals within my command.

Among these brave men, feeble and exhausted by disease, tortured and mutilated by cruel wounds, I have never yet heard the first word of despair, the first sigh of regret, that they had given health and life to their country.

If we may judge of the spirit of those they have left at home, and who may yet be called to the field, by the heroic temper of these men, we have nothing to fear as to the result.

In the solemn verdict of the ballot, and the deadly conflict of battle, this Government of the people will be sustained.

I beg that you will accept for yourself, and convey to the members of the Convention over which you presided, my sincere thanks for the great honor which they did me in placing my name before the electors of New York for a position so responsible and distinguished as that of Governor of the State.

I am, sir, with great respect, truly yours,

JAMES S. WADSWORTH.

JAMES S. THAYER,

AT THE DEMOCRATIC STATE CONVENTION, AT TWEDDLE HALL, ALBANY, JANUARY 31, 1861.

See how James S. Thayer, amid general applause, thus declared the general purpose of the assembled Seymourites in that Tweddle Hall Convention:

"We can, at least (said Thayer), by discussion, enlighten, settle and concentrate the public sentiment in the State of New York upon this question, *and save it from that fearful current, that circuitously, but certainly, sweeps madly on through the narrow gorge of 'the enforcemevt of the laws,' to the shoreless ocean of civil war.* [Cheers.] *Against this, under all circumstances, in every place and form, we must now and at all times oppose a resolute and unfaltering resistance.* The public mind will bear the avowal, and let us make it—*that if a revolution of force is to begin, it shall be inaugurated at home.* [Cheers.] And if the incoming administration shall attempt to carry out the line of policy that has been foreshadowed, we announce that when the hand of Black Republicanism turns to blood-red, and seeks from the fragments of the Constitution to construct a scaffolding for coercion—another name for execution—we will reverse the order of the French Revolution, and save the blood of the people by making those who would inaugurate a reign of terror the first victims of a national guillotine. [Enthusiastic applause.]

"The Democratic and Union party at the North made the issue at the last election with the Republican party, that, in the event of their success, and the establishment of their policy, the Southern States not only would go out of the Union, BUT WOULD HAVE ADEQUATE CAUSE FOR DOING SO. [Applause.]

"This is the position I took with 313,000 voters in the State of New York, on the 6th of November last. I shall not recede from it, having admitted that, in a certain contingency, *the Slave States would have just and adequate cause for a separation!* Now that the contingency has happened, I shall not withdraw that admission because they have been unwise or unreaonable in the 'time, mode and measure of redress.' [Applause.]

"What person, what right of property, what domestic right or privilege, what franchise, what security to life or liberty, is infringed by the rupture of the Federal relation between the States? [Applause.]

"But it is announced that the Republican Administration will enforce the laws against and in all the Seceding States. A nice discrimination must be exercised in the performance of this duty, not a hair's breadth outside the mark. You re member the story of William Tell, who, when he condition was imposed upon him to shoot an apple from the head of his own child, after he had performed the task let fall an arrow. 'For what is that?' said Gesler. 'To kill thee, tyrant, had I slain my boy!' [Cheers.] *Let one arrow winged by the Federal bow strike the heart of an American citizen, and who can number the avenging darts that will cloud the heavens in the conflict that will ensue?* [Prolonged applause.] What then is the duty of the State of New York? What shall we say to our people when we come to meet this state of facts? That the Union must be preserved. But if that cannot be, what then? PEACEABLE SEPARATION. [Applause.]"

So much for Thayer and his fellow-Seymourites in January, 1861.

Hon. Roscoe Conkling testifies that, when the proceedings of that Tweddle Hall Democratic Convention reached Washington, Keitt of South Carolina (already an open disunionist) exultingly proclaimed: "*There will be more men in New York alone to fight for us than the whole North can put down!*" Consider that Fernando Wood was then our Mayor, and had just formally proposed the secession of our city from the State, with a view to uniting her destinies with those of the pirate Confederacy, and that every Democrat hereabout then deprecated "coercion."

HAMILTON FISH.

The Hon. HAMILTON FISH, having been invited to preside over the recent Mass Meeting at Cooper Institute to ratify the nomination of the WADSWORTH and TREMAIN ticket, responded as follows:

GARRISON'S, Putnam Co., Oct. 9, 1862.

MY DEAR SIR: Your note inviting me to preside at the ratification meeting held last evening at the Cooper Institute, reached me here late last evening, after the hour for which the meeting was called. Of course I could neither be with you nor return an answer. I beg now to return you my thanks for the invitation, and especially for the kind personal desire expressed by you for its acceptance.

It is probable that, had the invitation been received sooner, I should not have been able to dispense with a business engagement here. At any rate, the meeting lost nothing by my absence. But I am most earnestly with those who wish the most vigorous prosecution of the war, to the utter overthrow of the last vestige and sign of rebellion.

It is time—high time—that this war be conducted on war principles—that the velvet glove with which we have been handling rebellion and treason be replaced by the mailed gauntlet, and that the Government avail itself of all the means and usages recognized by modern and civilized warfare to weaken and break down its enemies. It is a wasteful exhaustion of the means and power of the Nation, a wicked oppression upon the citizens, and cruelty to all, to tamper with the stern realities that are upon us, and to talk "Peace! peace! when there is no peace."

No, we have to *conquer* a peace—we cannot buy it, and if we could it would be valueless, as it would be disgraceful.

In the field, stern, sharp and active war; and in the council, stern, sure and quick justice, are the surest paths to an early, honorable and enduring peace.

Disloyalty and treason are not wholly confined to the South, and if traitors have not been persecuted, if spies have not been hanged, and if deserters have not been shot, it has not been for want of subjects.

With active war, the nation needs also equally active justice. The exemplary punishment of a few disloyal men, the hanging of a few spies, and the shooting of a few deserters, would have a most salutary influence, and would afford a most welcome and much needed assurance of earnestness in the search of peace in the proper direction—worth all the incarcerations (numerous as they have been) in Forts Lafayette and Warren, and elsewhere, and effective beyond all the "oaths of allegiance" that the ingenuity of man can devise, or that all the officers of the Government can administer in a lifetime. In times like these there is virtue in hemp and cold lead judiciously and judicially administered, and we have experienced grievous cruelty and wrong in excessive leniency shown to the guilty.

But pardon me, my dear sir, for this digression into which I have been unconsciously drawn. I did not intend to do more than explain to you, personally, the omission of a reply to your note, and I find myself talking on other matters. So I stop in the middle, and add assurances of the respect of Yours very truly,

HAMILTON FISH.

JAMES A. BRIGGS, Esq., New York.

www.ingramcontent.com/pod-product-compliance
Lightning Source LLC
LaVergne TN
LVHW020635110826
845149LV00004B/1212

9781418191009